CHANGE YOUR LIFE AND BE A BETTER PERSON

CHANGE YOUR LIFE AND BE A BETTER PERSON

TABLE OF CONTENTS

INTRODUCTION 3
CHAPTER 1 5
   CHANGE YOUR LIFE AND BE A BETTER PERSON 5
CHAPTER 2 8
   SELF-IMPROVEMENT - 5 QUESTIONS YOU SHOULD ASK YOURSELF TO BE A BETTER PERSON 8
CHAPTER 3 10
   SEVEN THINGS YOU CAN DO THAT WILL MAKE YOU A BETTER PERSON ... 10
CHAPTER 4 15
   PERSONAL GROWTH - HOW TO BE A BETTER PERSON IN YOUR 40'S AND 50'S ... 15
CHAPTER 5 19
   HOW TO BECOME A BETTER PERSON THROUGH EXERCISE 19
CHAPTER 6 24
   WHAT MUM DIDN'T TELL YOU ABOUT BEING A BETTER PERSON, STARTING RIGHT NOW! 24
CHAPTER 7 28
   HOW TO BE A BETTER HUSBAND TO MY WIFE (BE A WINSOME MAN) - CREATE STRONG FOUNDATION OF ATTRACTION 28
CHAPTER 8 34
   HOW TO BE A BETTER PERSON FOR OUR NATION 34
CHAPTER 8 37
   TOP TEN RESOLUTIONS TO BECOMING A BETTER PERSON 37
CHAPTER 9 41
   LEARN HOW TO TRICK THE MIND AND BECOME A BETTER PERSON 41
CHAPTER 11 44
   A MONTHLY TRIP TO A BEAUTY SALON CAN MAKE YOU A BETTER PERSON ... 44
CONCLUSION 47

INTRODUCTION

If you want to become a better person and achieve your full potential, you need to know which path to follow. With the right advice, you can help yourself grow and become the person that you have always wanted to be. To learn more about following the path of personal development, keep reading.

Try to be as selfless as you can. If you are always focused on your own needs and what is best for you, you may weaken many of your relationships and fail to grow as a person. It may seem paradoxical, but the less you focus on yourself and the more you focus on other people, the more quickly you will improve.

Try to find something positive in every aspect of your life. Even if it is just something as seemingly insignificant as appreciating the sunset, the more you seek out the positive, the more positive your life will be. Even when things look bad, you should still try to look for the silver lining.

In everything that you do, strive for perfection. You may never be able to reach true greatness, but if you set that as your goal, you will get closer than you ever thought possible. Do not be afraid of setting your sights too high. It is better to aim too high than to betray yourself by never trying at all.

The world is full of great wisdom that can help guide you on your path to true fulfillment, so seek out this knowledge and try to absorb it. True wisdom can be found on many different paths, so do not limit yourself to a single way of thought. Explore as many different ideas as you can so that you can gain the most benefit from the wisdom of humanity.

Being honest and consistent in your actions and beliefs is vital if you want to achieve greatness. If you say one thing but do another, you are not only betraying other people, but yourself as well. Try to make all of your words and deeds reflect your basic principles. Do not be afraid to stand up for what you believe is right, even in the face of mockery or anger.

Knowing who you really are is one of the most important parts of personal development. Until you develop enough self-awareness to understand your true identity, you will not be able to find the direction and guidance you need to reach your true potential. Explore your inner self until you are able to identify your core identity.

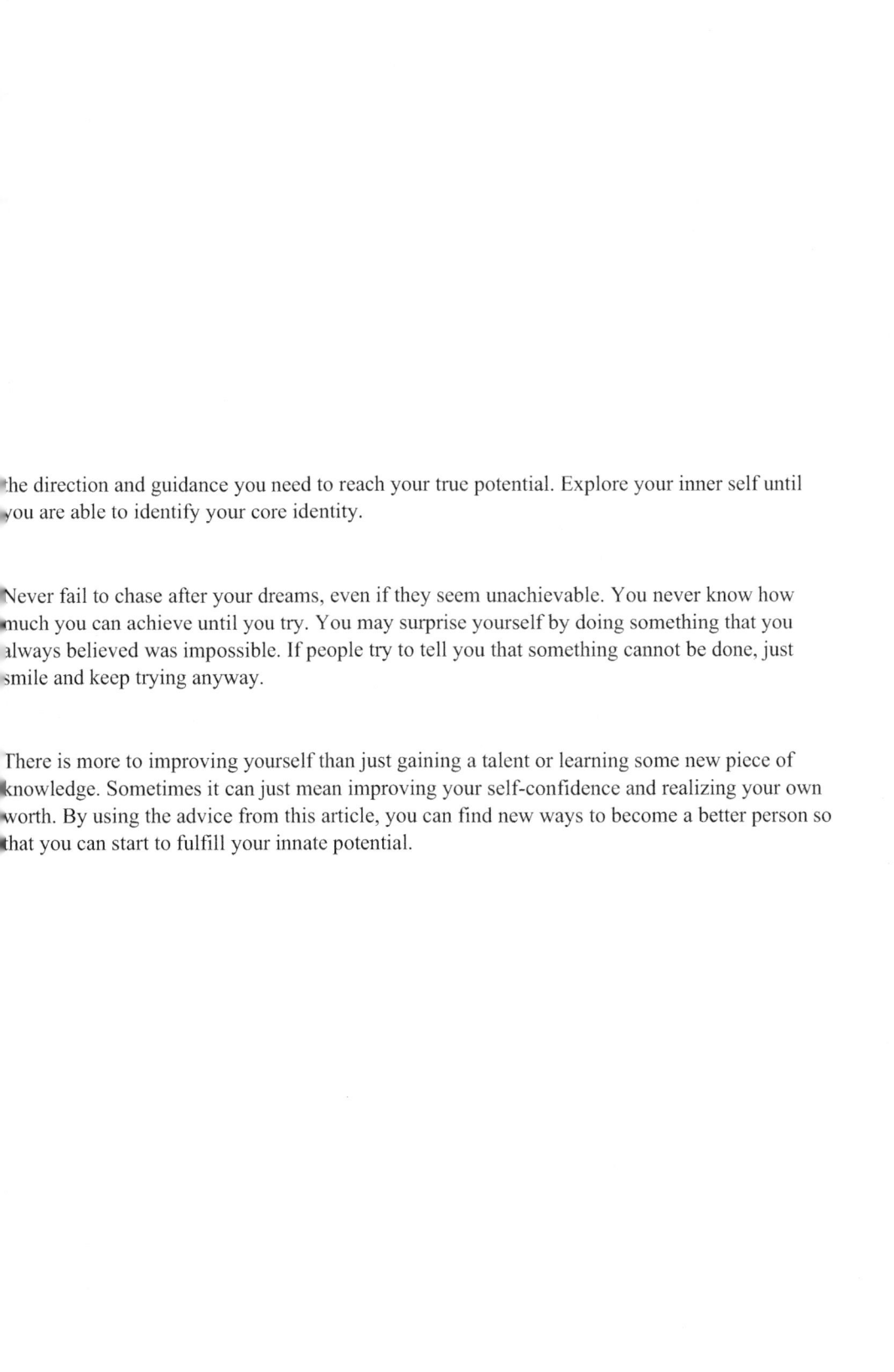

Never fail to chase after your dreams, even if they seem unachievable. You never know how much you can achieve until you try. You may surprise yourself by doing something that you always believed was impossible. If people try to tell you that something cannot be done, just smile and keep trying anyway.

There is more to improving yourself than just gaining a talent or learning some new piece of knowledge. Sometimes it can just mean improving your self-confidence and realizing your own worth. By using the advice from this article, you can find new ways to become a better person so that you can start to fulfill your innate potential.

CHAPTER 1

CHANGE YOUR LIFE AND BE A BETTER PERSON

I wish to be a better person and work hard at doing so. I read books to improve my understanding of self, finances, health, relationships and life in general. I do everything I can to implement the new information that I acquire.

Finding a balance between learning and taking action to change your life can be a challenge though. For some of us we can get stuck in a paralysis analysis mode. Constantly reading, going to seminars, speaking with counselors, coaches and the like, can lead to years of study, with few results other than an increased perspective.

After all we want to have more than just more knowledge and wisdom in life. We want to be prosperous and really LIVE life. No one wants to simply survive.

We all have our own learning perspective and understand life a little differently. There in lies some of the problems that we face in life. If you have the perspective that "Others are out to get you" then you will see a world of deceit, backbiting, scarcity, fear, and will live life accordingly. The actions of others will always be seen as a means to put you down, as though they are attacking you. You will then go about trying to defend yourself.

The great news here is that this is the opposite of how life really is and you can change your experience in life very easily by changing your core beliefs. Those beliefs are what lead to the thoughts you have and in turn the actions you take. If you have a negative perspective then your actions are in fact leading acting contrary to the thoughts of living a more prosperous, loving, happy, and enjoyable life.

The universal law of attraction is always at work and if you are feeding it the thought that others are out to get you, then your mind is going to work in exactly the manner necessary to make that your experience. So change your life by changing your thoughts.

If you have ever asked yourself how to change your life you need look no further than the very beliefs you hold to be true. If these beliefs are not empowering you to live a more fruitful life then what good are they doing you? Even if you say your being a realist you are doing nothing more than deceiving yourself. It may have helped protect your precious self worth up to this point yet that is really all.

Change your beliefs to something more positive, accept responsibility for life as it is and know that you made it that way and can change it for the better. You are good enough as you are, worthy of the very best in life.

3 TIPS TO BECOME A BETTER PERSON

I believe that most people want to become a better person in their life. No matter how bad the things they did in the past, if they are willing to change, people should accept them. To become a better person, it all depends on your determination, commitment and hard work. Therefore, if you are thinking of how to become a better person, you should apply the techniques mentioned below.

Tip 1 - Know your mistake

In order to become a better person, you should learn to identify your mistakes. Think or write it down what are those things that you did wrong in and the things that your friend dislike about you. After that, you should analyse the mistake you have done and try to avoid repeating it again and again. I do understand that it will be very hard for you to avoid it from the start. Therefore, you should give yourself some time, patient and courage to overcome and change.

Tip 2 - Learn from your mistake

I believed that most of the people have done something wrong and have offended or hurt someone else feeling. So, the second step you have to do to become a better person is to learn from our past mistake. It is common that you find it very hard to apologize to them if they belong to the group of people whom you do not like or from your work place. But if you do apologise to them, they will have an impression that you are trying to change and hope to get a second chance from them. And as time goes by, they will accept you.

Tip 3 - Forget the past and think for the future

Things that are done cannot be undone. Thus, it is impossible for us to delete away the wrong things we had done in the past. Therefore, the best way is to forget about the past and thinking of your future. You should start preparing for your future by doing good deeds. This will definitely help you to secure your future.

Therefore, if you really want to become a better person, you should start to be honest and treat people with sincerity. Do not judge them or criticise them as it will harm your relationship with them. If you have the intention and determination to change and become a better person, becoming a better person is not a difficult task to accomplish.

CHAPTER 2

SELF-IMPROVEMENT - 5 QUESTIONS YOU SHOULD ASK YOURSELF TO BE A BETTER PERSON

We all want to be better human beings. Or at least, that is what we should want. Often the people that think they have no room for improvement are the ones that need the most work. Here are some important questions to ask yourself if you want to be a better person.

1. What Do I Desire?

It is hard to get what you want from life if you don't know what that is. But knowing what you want from life is not easy. From childhood through your adult life you will find people that volunteer what you should want. And they mean well. But the right answer for you is particular to you and is independent of what society or your parents or your mentors and friends may want. To answer this question requires real introspection. But the answer could not be more important to your growth as a human being. If you do not know what you want you have zero chance of achieving it.

2. How Should I Change Myself?

Is there some part of you that can change to help you achieve what you desire? Part of your mind will offer the immediate answer, "no." We are conditioned to believe that a series of external forces prevents us from achieving our wants. But if you really want to achieve what you desire, engage in true introspection and try to determine whether you have behaviors or traits that need to be changed to facilitate what you want from life. For instance, do you have a temper or a penchant for quitting when the going gets tough? These traits will hold you back but they can be changed. The first step is acknowledging that they exist.

3. Where Is the Silver Lining?

There are many unpleasant things that life can throw at you. But there usually is a bright side. Unfortunately, you are usually to near what is going on to appreciate the bright side. So whenever you are in a bad situation, spend some time to think about the silver lining. This does not make the bad go away, but it helps give you perspective so that you can constructively deal with the bad but retain the good.

4. Have I Left Something Undone?

Regrets sneak up on you, but they can be powerful and lasting feelings. Have you left something undone? Are there relationships with family or friends that have ended due to neglect or conflict? There absolutely is no time like the present to repair them. This goes beyond repairing relationships. Is there something you have always wanted to do but never had because of time or your social circumstances? In other words, have you checked off your "bucket list?" If not, do it now.

5. Is There Something I Need To Do For Someone Else?

One can accumulate professional accolades and wealth but these things often do not fulfill as human beings. A good question to ask yourself is whether there is something more you can be doing for your community or other human beings? Start with your personal life. Can you make meaningful contributions to your family and friends to further develop your relationships with them or to further them as people?

After you think about your immediate circles expand your view to your larger community. How can you contribute to your community to make it a better place for the people in it? Maybe this means volunteering coaching basketball at the local rec center or raising money for a local charity. Depending on your means, your contributions to the community can encompass larger acts of philanthropy.

If you want to be a better human being, ask these 5 questions of yourself and have the courage to give yourself honest answers. They may surprise you. But whatever the answers they will further your journey towards self-improvement.

CHAPTER 3

SEVEN THINGS YOU CAN DO THAT WILL MAKE YOU A BETTER PERSON

Everyone would like to be a better person -- someone who is liked and admired. And there are several things you can do that will help you achieve this. Seven of them are listed below.

- Become more patient
- Smile at people (particularly, strangers), and say "Hello"
- Listen better
- Compliment people
- Don't criticize or blame
- Do something nice for someone, just for the fun of it
- Mind your own business

Let's looks at them one at a time.

Become More Patient

Patience is a very desirable trait, and as you might expect, many people do not have it. It is something, however, that is worthwhile developing. If you don't have patience you will become annoyed, bothered, irritated, and frustrated easily. Little things will lead to arguments, yelling and hurt feelings. Patience gives you peace of mind, and a feeling of contentment.

Many situations lead to impatience: yelling children, long lines at the grocery store, heavy traffic, arguments, waiting at doctor's office, and so on. Any of them can easily make you become impatient and lose your temper. So, how do you develop patience? It takes time and practise; Although most people do not think of it as a skill, it is a skill and that means that you're not going to acquire it overnight. You will have to devote time and effort towards developing it. Furthermore, it may mean changing your mindset.

One of the first things you can do when you find you are becoming impatient is count to ten before you say anything -- in particular, before you lose your temper. Also, make up your mind to restrain yourself even if you feel stressful. Wait until you calm down.

Acceptance is also important. Accept things that you have no control over -- don't worry about them. Ask yourself: Is it really worth it to get annoyed? You likely have little control over the problem so it's not worth worrying about it. If you do, the only thing that will happen is that your blood pressure will go through the roof. So calm down, relax and accept the situation as much as you can.

Smile at People (particularly, strangers), and Say "Hello

Have you ever noticed how most people prefer to avoid making eye contact with other people. They prefer walking around with their head down, looking at the floor or sidewalk. You may also have noticed that when you are at a stop sign and a car pulls up beside you, the driver prefers to stay back a bit so he can't see you directly. Maybe he's worried that you might turn and smile at him.

A good habit to develop is to keep your head up and make eye contact with people in front of you. Smile at them. It may surprise you, but many will smile back if you take the initiative. If they look friendly, say "hello." Resolve to do this at least once a day. It will make you feel better when someone says "Hello, how are you?" back.

This applies tenfold when you see someone you know. Smile broadly as you greet them. Act as if they're your best friend.

Listen Better

Most people are not good listeners. They would rather talk than listen. I remember standing in a doorway looking at people seated at tables playing bridge where I would swear that everybody in the room was talking, and no one was listening. So becoming a better listener is another habit that will make you a better person. You may, in fact, lose out on a lot of important information by not listening properly. And being a good listener is more than not interrupting and finishing people's sentences. Like patience, it's also a skill.

Some of the things you should do to become a better listener are:

Make eye contact with the person who you are talking to

Let them finish talking before you say anything.

Give them your complete attention.

When asked a question, respond immediately, and don't suddenly change the topic.

Don't say, "Yes, I know... I know."

Don't say, "No, you've got it wrong."

Don't try to impress them with your answers.

Don't become distracted and begin doing something else.

Compliment People

Everyone likes a compliment, and most people get very few. Furthermore, most people are very appreciative of compliments when they get them. In many cases it makes their day.

How often do you compliment people? Not often, I'd guess. Many people feel too embarrassed to compliment someone. But there's no doubt that giving a compliment pays dividends. The person receiving it immediately feels more friendly towards you, and may compliment you back. In addition a compliment makes everyone feel good. Usually a large smile comes over their face.

It's important, however, to make sure the compliment is genuine, and you really mean it. A compliment that is not genuine could be taken as sarcasm.

Who should you compliment? Parents, spouses, children, friends and even complete strangers are all good candidates. You should, in fact, make a point of complimenting someone every day.

Don't Criticize or Blame

We all feel the urge occasionally to criticize someone. But it's a good idea to stop before you say anything and think about it. Remember that criticism hurts -- regardless of who it is directed at.

Ask yourself: What good is the criticism going to do? Who will it help? Anyone? There are, indeed, cases where mild criticism might help, but they are rare.

Some of the things that criticism leads to are: hurt feelings, anger, broken friendships, and fights. Indeed, there is only one of two things a person being criticized will do: He (or she) will retreat in shame and embarrassment and say little, or they will lash back at you in anger. Neither of these are in your best interest. So catch yourself when you feel an urge to criticize. Furthermore, if you criticize someone, you'll likely find that you end up feeling just as bad as the one you are criticizing.

Blaming someone is just as bad as criticizing. Many people feel frustrated when things don't go the way they want, and they immediately begin to blame someone. It's amazing, in fact, how many people blame their shortcomings on someone else. Many people blame their parents for their behavior; they blame them because they didn't finish school, or didn't go to university. Even criminals blame others for their behavior. In most cases, however, there's only one person to blame for your shortcoming, and it's you. You have to hold yourself responsible for everything you do; it's up to you to overcome any shortcomings you may have. Your choices were made by you (in almost all cases); they were not forced on you, so you have to take responsibility for them. Don't blame others.

Do Something Nice for Someone, Just for the Fun of it

How often do you go out of your way to do something nice for someone? In the case of most people, it's not very often. But doing something nice for someone will give you a warm feeling that will last all day, and maybe longer. The important thing is not to expect anything in return; in fact, don't even expect a "thank you," even though you'll likely get it. You've already got your reward: a feeling of satisfaction. In particular, don't get angry or annoyed if you don't get anything back. This will destroy everything..

What kind of things can you do? Think of your spouse, children, friends and neighbors. What do they need? Older people may need help with their yardwork. Take food to needy neighbors. Volunteer time to charity. Give someone money without them knowing where it came from. Donate old toys to children.

Helping other can reduce stress and add to your happiness.

Mind Your Own Business

Sticking your nose in where it's not needed, or belongs, can quickly backfire on you. In particular, don't try to tell people how to do things better (unless they ask for your advice). In many cases they'll resist your advice, even if it is good. This doesn't mean you shouldn't help people. You should. If someone is having a problem it's only common courtesy to help them. But if you see they are doing something the wrong way, don't make them look bad. And don't go around trying to solve everyone's problems.

Minding your own business also means not talking behind people's back or gossiping. Some people can't wait to tell others about some "juicy gossip" -- even when they're not sure it's true. Refrain from this.

CHAPTER 4

PERSONAL GROWTH - HOW TO BE A BETTER PERSON IN YOUR 40'S AND 50'S

As I am a weeks away from my 50th birthday, I am slightly more serious about my life and its direction at this time really than ever before. I'm contemplating what needs to stay with me as I cross the threshold and what can stay in my 40's. On my 49th birthday, I began my career as a life coach by starting my certification process. Six months later, I was certified and ready to start my practice. Intention perfect - success still in progress.

As we transition into our next chapter of our life story, what positive energies can we bring with us? And what baggage can be finally dumped and, mostly importantly, how do we do this easily and correctly. What should come with me?

My newfound dedication to making my needs a priority

My voice as I finally learn to speak up for myself and state what's important to me.

My continued passion to better myself with a wellness program, dedication to my relationship with God, mediation and learning everything I can be a more sophisticated life coach.

Having a job that I am enthusiastic about going to each day. I know that everyday at work can be a struggle as different personalities are merged together and expected work well. What can I do to bring positive energy into our workplace? Can I drop my judgment of others, Negative Nancy attitude and begin to attract more positive vibration so my co-workers can benefit from this attitude? What we think about is brought to us and what we resist, we get and what we don't like in others is probably what we don't like in ourselves.

If we're anxious about going to work, is it time for a change? If our feet are reluctant to enter that building and our thoughts are on dread, is our inner voice trying to communicate with us that it is time for a job change, new career direction. Hey listen, time will pass no later what. I remember speaking with a cousin a few years back, and he was thinking about going back to school to explore new career directions. His schooling would take about five years to complete. His attitude was perfect -- the five years will pass anyway so he might as well be doing something to better himself along the way. I loved this.

As our years pass, are we spending our years moving in the right direction? Is it time for a challenge or maybe we've been in a demanding position for many years and it's time to slow down and reap the rewards of our hard work.

We are what we make of ourselves. I am proud of the person I am becoming and I've absolutely enjoyed my experiences. Some for than others -- I'll be honest. I can put my head on my pillow each night with ease. I am so free from my old negative thinking, self-sabotaging ways. We are blessed with this life and as a coach; I want to help women move confidently into this new area of life. As the "Fab at 40" or the "Nifty at 50" group mature perfectly, what can we learn from each other's successes, milestones, strengths and determinations? Can we learn from our less-than strengths, setbacks and negativities?

If you could see into the next five years, what would you like to have accomplished? I met a friend the other day, and we was asking me about my practice and I told her happy I was that I dedicated this past year to become a life coach and I remarkable I felt with this accomplishment. She explained that she always wanted to be a nurse, but never got around to it because of one thing or another - kids, family, husband's career advancement, and complacency with her own career, comfort and need to take care of others before herself. When can it be her turn? Why can't it be now, but is she up to the challenge? That's what she needs contemplate and digest.

WHY NEGATIVE MEMORIES WILL NEVER TEACH YOU HOW TO BE A BETTER PERSON

You've heard many times that memories, no matter how good or bad they are, should be appreciated by you as a necessary part of living. Books, media, people or even your family repeat over and over again the same thing: "Keep your all memories, they are helping you in your spiritual development."

It sounds a bit mystic and a bit magical that traumatic events will help you so the only way is to suffer.

Just imagine for a moment: you are born on that beautiful planet - Earth. You are growing up as a happy child, open and spontaneous to learn and try everything to express your inner self.

Unfortunately, one day something bad happens to you. It turns out that your family is not a safe place for you anymore. You get a lot of abuse from your parents, children at school start bullying you and you are left alone with all of the pain and a broken heart.

Progressively, your mind is gathering more and more bad memories full of pain and inner emotional suffering.

You think, "Hmm... that is good, pain and trauma will teach me important life lessons, so one day I will spiritually evolve as a beautiful soul who will help other people in the world."

Unfortunately, that beautiful, idealized fantasy is never gonna happen.

Life starts to be very challenging. You naturally attract more trauma to your life where people easily hurt your vulnerable heart all the time.

What do you think about yourself? "I am a failure. I am unloved, unwanted. I don't deserve to be loved and respected."

You feel doomed in life and deeply feel that you missing a lot of life-force energy. Like it has been drained from your body and you live somewhere else, somewhere... outside of your body.

A negative polarity in your system makes you a bitter, cold-hearted person. Your heart is emotionally shut down because you are simply frightened of love and hurt from others.

Do you still think that keeping and remembering negative memories will teach you important life lessons, and how to be a better human?

Hmm... Wait a minute... It is impossible to forget your memories! Sometimes it happens, but you need a lot of time to do that. Then somehow you can forget about bad events and start living again as a happy person.

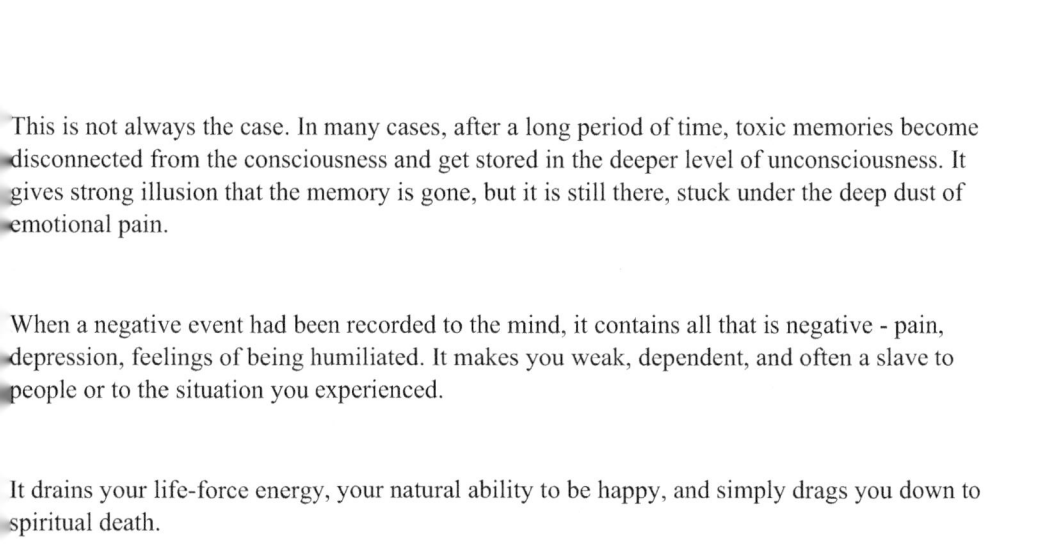

This is not always the case. In many cases, after a long period of time, toxic memories become disconnected from the consciousness and get stored in the deeper level of unconsciousness. It gives strong illusion that the memory is gone, but it is still there, stuck under the deep dust of emotional pain.

When a negative event had been recorded to the mind, it contains all that is negative - pain, depression, feelings of being humiliated. It makes you weak, dependent, and often a slave to people or to the situation you experienced.

It drains your life-force energy, your natural ability to be happy, and simply drags you down to spiritual death.

Luckily, now there is a way out from that pathetic situation. There is a process where you can restore your natural flow of energy, get back to your body, erase negative events from your mind to where you feel positive, strong, self-empowered and enthusiastic for your future.

CHAPTER 5

HOW TO BECOME A BETTER PERSON THROUGH EXERCISE

It may seem like the easy option to stay on the sofa, in front of the TV, but the benefits of taking some regular exercise are so great, you'd be mad to ignore them. So stop making excuses and get out there or stay indoors if you prefer. There's something to suit every taste and ability when it comes to exercise. You may even find you enjoy it!

Improve your mental health

You don't need to be a top athlete to discover the positive effects of exercise on mood. There are the chemical changes that occur in the brain due to the stimulation of exercise. In the short-term, endorphins are released by the brain, which provides a mood booster that is maintained after the activity has ended.

The production of Dopamine, which affects mood, attention and learning is stimulated through exercise. Seratonin, known as the 'molecule of happiness' is also increased through physical exertion. Sleep quality, the ability to focus the mind and manage stress are all aspects of psychological wellbeing that are improved. It's also well known that debilitating conditions such as anxiety and depression can reduced through exercise.

Physical Rewards

The benefits of exercise are well documented and hard to ignore. It seems that almost every aspect of our physical health can be improved through exercise.

Take a look at these impressive lists for starters:

Improved:

bone density

liver function

circulation

digestion

libido

immune system

blood pressure

metabolism

heart function

flexibility

stamina

Reduced:

injury

proneness to infection and virus

osteoporosis

overweight

diabetes

There are also more subtle, but equally important physical changes to be expected, which include improved skin, hair, nails and muscle-tone. Is there any wonder that we begin to feel better about ourselves very quickly as we see a new, more toned, leaner body appearing with fewer spots and brighter skin?

The effect of exercise on self-esteem is immeasurable, and not only because of the changes to our appearance.

Through mastering a new skill or activity, we begin to think of ourselves differently and gain a new self-respect through sticking to the discipline of regular exercise. As confidence grows, so does the desire to socialize and join clubs or exercise classes, which in turn increases our chances of forming friendships with like-minded people. You may even meet your future partner through exercise or improve your relationships with loved ones through shared activities and interests.

Don't be put off by thinking that you must have the full kit and equipment as you can always hire or borrow until you know you're going to stick at something. If you decide on a chosen activity, it's definitely a worthwhile investment in the long rung and you usually only have to shell out once.

Fitness levels or weight can also put people off but there are plenty of gentle forms of exercise, which allow you to progress slowly and at your own pace, such as Yoga and Pilates. You can start by exercising to a DVD at home if reluctant to join a class or take a friend who'll give you added confidence to get started. There really is no excuse so get going today!

5 STEPS TO BECOMING A HAPPIER AND BETTER PERSON

The people who achieve the highest levels of success and happiness in life are both thankful for what they have yet constantly seek ways to improve. If you want to be one of these people here are 5 things you may want to do:

Rethink Your Money - Is money a major factor in every decision you make? If so you are not in control of your life - your money is. What this means is that you need to rethink the role money has in your life.

What should you do?

Stop spending all of it - Many people today spend 100% of their incoming paycheck. When they get a raise they get a bigger car or a bigger house or more expensive clothes. This is called living paycheck to paycheck and inevitably leads to anxiety and constant worry about money. Fight the need to constantly upgrade your material possessions, and focus on being happy with what you already have.

Don't be cheap - Although you should be downsizing on your material possessions, don't skimp on the fun stuff. With the extra money you should now find yourself with feel free to treat yourself and others. Spend that extra $10 on the lobster or on dessert. Instead of taking your mom to Denny's for her birthday, take her somewhere really nice and don't be afraid to spurge a little. In other words, when something comes up that you really want to do - do it!

Cutting back spending on material possessions, while increasing spending on fun activities will add a new dimension of happiness to your life.

Don't sweat the small stuff - It's all small stuff. Have you ever gotten totally worked up over a co-worker's, a friend's or a family member's behavior. Don't! When you get angry this isn't a reflection on anybody except YOU. When you yell and scream and your blood temperature starts to rise you're really just demonstrating to the world the lack of control you have over your own life.

What should you do?

Be the better person. Realize that everyone in this world is simply dealing with life the best way they know how. If someone is being selfish or hurtful towards you they are doing so out of some form of fear or lack in their own life. So don't let yourself get caught up in the battle.

Take responsibility for everything in your life, both positive and negative. It's a liberating experience once you accept 100% responsibility for everything that happens to you and your reaction to it.

Socialize - One of the greatest predictors of health and happiness is how social you are. When was the last time you did something fun with a group of friends just for the fun of it? If you're not doing something enjoyable with others at least once a week then it's time for that to change.

What should you do?

Join a social group that has common interests as you.

Make time for your activities. Most people site "lack of time" as the reason they don't have more fun in life. Your social time is paramount to your well being and should be equally important as your job and your family responsibilities.

Exercise regularly. We all know the benefits of exercise, so why not make regular exercise a part of your social activities.

Give - A person is measured by what they give not what they have. To give is to say to the world and to yourself: "I have more than everything I need to be happy". You can be a giver at any age, in any situation, and at any income level.

What should you do?

Give your money - Learning to be comfortable giving money is not easy. However, once you realize that money ultimately has little importance you may find yourself with a little something extra. Resist the urge to buy a useless luxury item, instead donate it to a cause that needs it more than you do.

Give your time - Volunteering is a way to give and become more social.

Seize opportunities - Life is a series of opportunities to make the world a better place. Which ones you take and which ones you pass up speaks volumes about who you are as a person.

Practice Self Improvement - Make self-improvement a regular fixture in your life. Like learning anything, becoming a better person isn't an overnight change, it takes practice. What should you do?

Research - Research the art of self-improvement. Read books, watch videos, go to seminars. The transformation won't be overnight but with effort you WILL become the person you want to be.

Turn every setback into a lesson - Life presents us with challenges and sometimes we fail. When this happens, don't complain and don't blame someone else. Instead treat every failure as an opportunity to get better, to do better, and to be better.

CHAPTER 6

WHAT MUM DIDN'T TELL YOU ABOUT BEING A BETTER PERSON, STARTING RIGHT NOW!

Do you want to be a better person but don't really know where, or how to start? It is easier than you think and there are a number of things you can do to get started. Do something nice today to make yourself, and others feel better. Here are some suggestions that you can get started with right away!

Say something friendly to someone you meet and try to smile and look happy. Turn off that critical voice in your head and start talking friendly without yourself as well.

If you have the chance, take the initiative and talk to someone who is new, or shy, in school or at work. Invite them out for a coffee, or lunch.

Help someone who needs it when you get a chance. For example, help an elderly person across the street, or offer to carry their shopping bags for them.

Let someone pass you in line, or in traffic.

Dare to change the topic when others begin to gossip, or talk about someone else behind their back. Walk a way or let them know you are not OK with talking about other people behind their backs.

Write a letter of appreciation to an organization or social movement that you think actually do make a difference, and some good in the world!

Work on your listening skills. This is a big one for me and I really try to remind myself on a daily basis to be a better listener. I have a friend who is a really good listener, and to be able to give another person the gift of your total presence and concentration when they are talking is great!

Tell a few inspiring and encouraging things to another person every day, and as many as possible to yourself.

Open the door for someone. It is said that for every time that you open a door for someone, seven others do the same thing.

Start writing a gratitude journal or joy report. Take a moment every night before going to sleep to think about your day and write down the things that made you happy and grateful.

Turn off the autopilot. Take a walk or go for a ride and think about how you really want to live. What characteristics do you want to develop? How do you want to be towards, respond to and treat other people? How can you contribute to make the world a better place?

The selfish reason to choose goodness

More and more scientific studies are showing that goodness is actually something that pays of. When we are generous a pleasure center in the brain gets activated that gives us a good experience from treating other people well. It is related to the same pleasure centers that gets activated by good food, sex or drugs. And as with all pleasure, it is addictive.

SIX TIPS FOR CLOSE AND INTIMATE RELATIONSHIPS - HOW TO BE A BETTER FRIEND AND LOVER IN THE NEW YEAR

So here we are at the threshold of a new year and decade. No doubt many are making out their lists of grand resolutions to improve their lives over the next year. At or near the top of most of those lists will be the expressed desire to cultivate closer and more intimate relationships. This article provides seven tips on how to become a better friend and lover in the coming year.

To Be a Better Friend and Lover Become a Better Listener

The first tip to become to cultivate close and intimate relationships is to improve your listening skills. Most people want to share about themselves and few have learned the fine art of listening. Listening is a participation sport. It is not merely sitting passively by as the other person rambles on about this and that. To listen well means to be actively engaged with consistent eye contact, summarizing the thoughts shared, and asking clarifying question.

To Improve Your Friendships and Love Life Spend Time with the Other Person

The second tip to cultivate close and intimate relationships is to make time in your calendar. The depth of a friendship or love life depends on the amount of quality and quantity time you spend with that other person.

To Be a Better Friend and Lover Strengthen the Emotional Bond

Spending time together is one thing; spending meaningful time together that strengthens the emotional bond takes creative planning. A third tip to cultivate close and intimate relationships is to plan dates or get-togethers that engage all five senses and provide an experience beyond the ordinary or mundane.

To Improve Your Friendships and Love Life Learn a New Conflict Resolution Skill

Conflict is a normal part of close relationships and can be conduits for even greater intimacy. So, the fourth tip for more intimate and meaningful relationships is to learn a new skill on how to handle conflict more constructively. If you need tips on how to creatively deal with tense situations, there are many wonderful resources online or in the bookstore including The Magic of Making Up .

To Be a Better Friend and Lover Give Unexpected Gifts at Unexpected Times

This tip comes from the movie Finding Forrester and especially applies to guy/girl relationships. In the movie the older character William Forrester tells his young counterpart that "the key to a woman's heart is an unexpected gift at an unexpected time." Of course to give a gift that will make an impact, you will need to know what kind of unexpected gift will truly move your friend or lover's heart. This means you have to spend time with them and carefully listen to them.

To Improve Your Friendships and Love Life Touch Others in Appropriate Ways

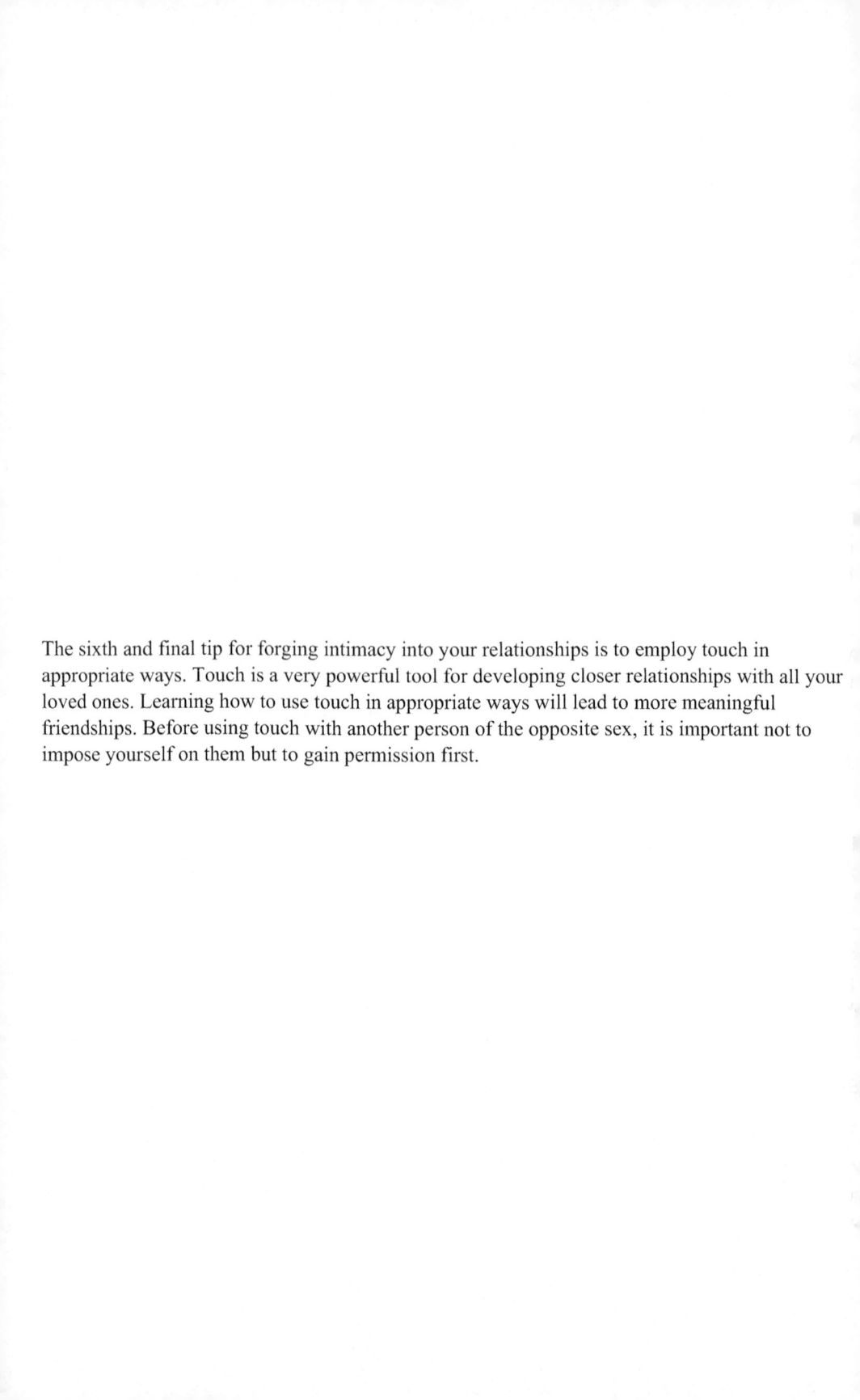

The sixth and final tip for forging intimacy into your relationships is to employ touch in appropriate ways. Touch is a very powerful tool for developing closer relationships with all your loved ones. Learning how to use touch in appropriate ways will lead to more meaningful friendships. Before using touch with another person of the opposite sex, it is important not to impose yourself on them but to gain permission first.

CHAPTER 7

HOW TO BE A BETTER HUSBAND TO MY WIFE (BE A WINSOME MAN) - CREATE STRONG FOUNDATION OF ATTRACTION

If you want to be a better husband to your wife then you have to be a winsome man and reform your persona. The mistake men make when they try to be a better husband is they do not create strong foundation of attraction. They act like a boy in relationship, instead of being a masculine winsome man.

These days wives are tired of playing the role of mommy. They are exhausted from acting like a mom of their husband. It is against their nature to make all the plans in the relationship and act like a husband.

According to wives, it is tough to find the traits of an actual winsome man in a husband. They never feel undeniable sexual attraction for their husband in long-term relationship.

How To Be A Better Husband To My Wife?

The winsome quality of your persona is the most important thing for your wife. So, for being a better husband, first you need to work on your own persona and make yourself worthy.

Here are my few secrets which not only projected me as a better husband to my wife but also ignited the sexual intensity in my relationship. I doubled the sexual desire of my wife for me with these below secrets.

Be A Winsome Man.

A winsome man is a man with high status and high values. He knows that high status is a major turn on for women. Besides, high status embodies the social status of a person. Especially for women, high social status can be only acquired by high status.

You not only articulate your dominance with high status but also assign yourself like an authoritative masculine man. Let me tell you, a man with high social status is a sexually powerful man for women.

Women judge you from your social status.

In addition, a wife utterly surrenders herself in front of a sexually powerful man and does everything in her power to keep her man happy.

Now, how to project yourself like a winsome man who is authoritative, masculine and sexually powerful?

Fortunately, you do not need money for being a winsome man. Here are few best ways to show yourself like a winsome man.

1. Do Friendship with imperial and decisive people.

Do friendship with fashion designers, restaurant managers, entrepreneurs, sportsmen, meteorologists, and firefighters etc. Your wife observes your personality by watching at your social status. So, avoid being with low status people. Enrich your social status and keep authoritative and decisive people around you in order to make your wife drool over you.

2. Women Love The Masculinity Of Men.

If you want to be a better husband to your wife then you have to be a masculine man and avoid acting like a boy. A masculine man treats her wife like a ravishing lady and give her very special treatment.

He handles tough situation calmly; He keeps his emotions in control; He achieves his targets passionately; He Holds confident body language; He never panics; He speaks slowly through his chest; He is an action taker man and he solves problem quietly rather than complaining about it.

In addition, a masculine winsome man is always the best dressed man in the room. He is financially intelligent and dominates the attention of people with his interesting conversation skills. For a wife, this type of masculine winsome husband is the best.

3. Women Rate Sexually Powerful Man As Sexy.

You have to be a sexually powerful man for being a better husband. A sexually powerful man is a sexually adventurous person. His acts, traits, and persona always convince a woman to do passionate sex with him. His sexual passion makes her wife go crazy for him.

If you want to be a sexually powerful man then you have to do plenty of things. For example, give your wife sexy silk thong, take her dancing, give her massage, be expert in foreplay, learn sex skills and provide her orgasms etc.

You will be worshipped by your wife always if you will transform yourself into a sexually powerful man and satisfy your wife in bed with your amazing sex skills.

These above tips are vital for being a better husband. Being a better husband is not only about giving your wife flowers or taking her to dinners; it is all about being a winsome man. Follow these above tips for making your wife chase you entire life.

HOW TO BE A BETTER WIFE - TIPS FOR KEEPING YOUR HUSBAND

Do you argue with your husband most of the time, even about petty things? Does your husband spend more time with the office rather than at home? Is your relationship with your husband on the brink of breaking up? If you answered yes to all the questions, don't panic.

While there is no such thing as a "perfect marriage", learning how to be a better wife can definitely help. Oftentimes, husbands feel neglected by their wives because of changes in priorities - either be it the kids, or a career. Being married is one thing, but staying married takes a lot of work.

When you feel that your husband is drifting away from you, read the tips below on how to be a better wife.

Tip 1: Respect.

Respect is the key to a successful husband and wife tandem. As much as possible, talk to your husband calmly. Everything can be discussed without having to nag or raise your voice, even when you're upset about something. Do not mock or belittle your husband, especially in front of family and friends. Constant communication with your hubby will help you how to improve and how to be a better wife. When you give your husband the respect he deserves, you're bound to get the same from him.

Tip 2: Give him personal space.

Just as women look forward to "me" time, guys also have instances wherein they want to do stuff they enjoy. Especially when your husband is the only one working for your family, chances are he has a lot of pressure on his back. Your husband has a great deal of stress in providing for your family's needs so it's no surprise that he will look for personal space. Hanging out with friends, indulging in a particular sport or hobby, or just as simple as watching TV will help him de-stress and relieve him from burden for the time being. Make sure that you give him time to relax and unwind. He'll love you for that.

Tip 3: Stay attractive.

Looking your best all the time for your husband is also a major consideration on how to be a better wife. You should not stop wearing nice dresses and sexy lingerie once you're married. Staying attractive doesn't mean wearing make up all the time. Keep your skin healthy or wear nice clothes will surely make your husband drool at the sight of you while you're preparing dinner. And when it's time for bed, wear seductive sleepwear and a perfume he loves on you so you can enjoy the night together.

Tip 4: Keep the love alive.

It is common for couples to stop being sweet and romantic after a several years of being married. If you're thinking of ways on how to be a better wife, showing how much you love your husband should be a priority. Surprise him by cooking his favorite dish, leave a note on his wallet, or set a date where the two of you can catch a movie or just spend some time together.

HOW TO BE A BETTER GIRLFRIEND SO HE'LL LOVE YOU EVEN MORE - MUST READ ADVICE FOR YOU!

Is it possible to learn how to be a better girlfriend? It is! We can all learn something new that will enhance our relationships. When a woman stops trying to grow and better herself, her boyfriend may become bored or tired of the monotony. You can do some very simple things that will ensure that you're the best girlfriend you possibly can be. The bonus of that is your guy will feel even closer to you and your relationship will be the strongest it's ever been.

Here are a few tips on how to be a better girlfriend:

Don't allow jealousy to enter your relationship. Jealousy is a common human emotion. You're bound to experience it if the man you adore is hanging out with a beautiful woman. However, jealousy speaks more of your insecurities than it does of his behavior. If you overreact whenever he's around a pretty girl, he'll think you have no confidence in yourself. It will wear on him if you argue with him over the women he works with or the fact he spends times with female friends. Men long to be with a woman who isn't jealous at all. Become her and he'll want you endlessly.

Don't be overly dramatic, ever. You really need to understand this point if you hope to be a better partner for your boyfriend. Men aren't keen on drama. They don't like it and it makes them uncomfortable. If you make a huge deal out of every small thing your boyfriend will soon tire of you. Men want to be with women who are carefree and easy going. Let the little things go. Don't question him about his feelings constantly and he'll appreciate it always.

Don't try and change anything about him. Your boyfriend probably likes himself just as he is. If you love him, you shouldn't be thinking about asking him to change anything. He wants and needs to be accepted just as he is. You need that from him too in relation to yourself. If you ensure that he knows that you adore him and all his flaws, he'll open up and they'll be an even tighter emotional bond between the two of you.

The key to learning how to be a better girlfriend is to understand how to be a better person in general. Be kind, considerate and loving. He'll see the best in you if you allow it to always shine through.

CHAPTER 8

HOW TO BE A BETTER PERSON FOR OUR NATION

Skimming through the TV channels last night, I glimpsed through the Indian movie "Rang de Basanti". It is a blockbuster flick which became another mark of success for Amir Khan. A story which certainly goes directly to the heart has a deep message behind it. Bless the racism germs running wildly in my blood since birth; I am not a huge fan of Indian movies among many of their products. However this movie couldn't impress me more. I have viewed this film couple of times before but last night it got me into thinking. It was thoughts which shook me from inside and I couldn't help but penning them down.

For those who haven't watched the movie here is the story for it would be difficult to follow without knowing the story. This movie "Rang de Basanti" is about 6 friends who lost their friend at the hands of corrupt politicians and government officials. The friends, students of a university, now set on the course to change the system. They are faced with hurdles and obstacles but their determination triumphs showing them the path of their course. For the rest of the story you will have to watch the movie.

During the course of their journey of changing the country prevailing system these students kills the Defense Minister. Now what struck me as stunning was the extent to which these students were prepared to go for achieving their goals. At this point many of you might argue this was merely a movie and it was recorded according to a well decided script. However if we eliminate this argument for the time being and believe this movie was basically a real story recorded then we will discover a very disturbing nature of humans. Being a university student I couldn't imagine myself going to the heights the 6 friends went to achieve their goal. It was at this time I realized this unsettling fact about human nature. These 6 six friends had faced a very huge loss in the shape of their close friend. They were numb with the pain of this unbearable loss and it was this loss which was feeding their strength and determination. The idea of pain strengthening the determination of a person may sound absurd but this is the unbelievable fact. The person who is satisfied with life turns immune and insensitive to the problems of others. With the passage of time this person is encased in a shell turning him blind and deaf to the issues related with those around him as he is bothered only about himself. Now this shell will only be broken when he will be faced with a loss of great magnitude. Only after bearing the loss the person appreciates the problems of life and lives life in the truest sense.

Now if we look at ourselves with a criticizing eye to uncover the truth about us then we would realize that we are being encased in that impenetrable shell with each passing second. The condition of our country is far worse than we can even imagine. If we would start enumerating the problems or rather the visible signs that will eventually lead to the failure of our country then maybe an entire book could be written on it. However the thing to be borne in our minds should be that it is all down to us to take care of our country. Instead of being encased in a shell and simply caring for ourselves only if we could commence with the idea of working for all the people around us then visible signs of progress could be observed.

Our ailing country needs this medicine from our hands. It's the least we can do to put our country back on the right path. This doesn't need any huge sacrifices from us. All we would be required to do would be to think about the greater good. Take a minute and sit back to analyze how far we have come on the road of selfishness. Everyday our latest model wide screen television updates us about some doctor's malpractice leading to death of a poor man's child. Everyday on traffic signals we watch without a care children begging while we sit in our air-conditioned cars waiting for the signal to turn green. Almost everyday we hear news about someone succumbing to suicide as life had gotten tough for him. We see our brothers in the Army fighting brutally with their brothers in remote villages and other sparsely populated areas. We see mutilated dead bodies of our brothers who became the victim of suicide attacks. Now how long will we continue to stand as bystanders, acting to be aggrieved over the sorrows and losses of others? How long will it be before we stand up to take some action over the loss of our brothers? Does an only blood relation matter to us? Are we free from bonds tying us to the people of same nationality, religion, race etc? Just analyze this personal event to see our height of selfishness. I was sitting with couple of my friends when one, after reading a SMS, said three people are dead in a suicide bomb attack today. The other friend asked was it in Karachi? On hearing the reply in negative the friend exclaimed a sigh in relief. This event merely goes to show that just because this condemning event didn't take place in our home city so we shouldn't be bothered by it. Plainly speaking unless we face a loss bereaving us of our personal possession or relations we would continue to be immune and careless to the worries of others.

We have all transformed into self-occupied machines that are running wildly after personally set worldly goals and objectives. We are suffering diseases like diabetes, depression, migraine and numerous others which have made our lives miserable. Instead of pondering over the reasons of these ailments we trust the medicines. The reality is that we are destroying the human traits. In other words we are quitting being human anymore.

Even at this point my mind is over-flowing with ideas and my fingers want to keep writing but I guess that would be digressing from my topic. To surmise I believe it would be more than sufficient if we all try to live as human beings are supposed. Simply by replacing self-interest with care of humanity we could change the course of this country. All we need to realize is that simply by performing our duties, whatever they may be, with sincerity and devotion we will be contributing to the betterment of our homeland and the world at large. Lets end with the hope that the moment of awakening approach us before we have to face any personal losses.

CHAPTER 9

TOP TEN RESOLUTIONS TO BECOMING A BETTER PERSON

So this year you have everything you want. The one thing you need is something your friends and family have been wishing for years, for you to become a better person. So you swear too much, you fart too loud, you laugh at homeless people on the street, but God loves you right?

Well God has been rumored to be just putting up with people like you, plus he is on another plane so has the option of tuning you out. Your friends, family and co-workers have to see you all the time, and they deserve a little relief too.

Being more cultured is the no# 1 resolution for this year. Would it be nice to surprise your girlfriend with tickets to a play instead of the WWF? Wouldn't it feel good to comment on a particular Authors newest works instead of quoting from a marvel comic?

This list will start you on your way to becoming a better person in the New Year.

About 50% of all people accomplish their new year's resolutions. With these ten insightful concepts you only need to accomplish half of them to be well on your way to being a high cultured, well mannered, compassionate, well though of citizen.

These resolutions were created in part, from a poll of upper class New Years Eve Partiers whom were asked if they could change something abut who they are what would be the first thing to go? Following these resolutions will set you on your way to a much more satisfying year.

Here goes.

Start saying this list out loud with the phrase "I Will..." in front of each resolution. Go on now.

Top Ten Resolutions to becoming a better person.

Become more cultured

Eat more vegetables

See more plays

Get in Shape

Give more money

Have more fun

Learn to Sing

Have Better Sex

Read more books

Swear less

Set your resolution goals now and be on your way to being a much better person. Bookmark this page now and come back often and see if you are better than you were last year.

MEDITATION HELPS YOU TO BECOME A BETTER PERSON

Do you feel heavy, unsatisfied or even tired often these days? Are you not really happy with your life? Or do you take immense stress these days? It all points down to one positive and practical solution, meditation. Meditation can help solve most of your stress and with daily practice; you can actually feel peace and start to solve all your problems yourself one by one.

Meditation is all about quieting your minds, positively. It's not easy but it's worth it. You need to do it right. All you have you to do is to become positive and let that positivity lead you to become a better person.

A "better person" is good at personal, professional and spiritual level. So how do you start to meditate? Glad, you asked. To imagine the power of meditation, you must know that meditation has been practiced for thousands of years. Earlier it was used to deepen understanding of sacred and mystical forces of life. In this era, it is better known for relaxing and stress management.

Meditating is a medicine for mind; stress makes your head jumbled up with many thoughts. Meditation takes you to a deep relaxation state and tranquil mind.

Research yet again proves that regular meditation can certainly improve your health and with that meditation may help such conditions as:

- Allergies
- Depression
- Sleep problems
- Substance abuse
- Fatigue
- Heart disease
- Anxiety disorders
- Asthma
- High blood pressure
- Pain Binge eating
- Cancer

So you know meditation is really important for you and can tremendously help you in every way. So the real question is how do you meditate?

Ways to meditate can include:

- Guided meditation. It's all about visualization of your happy memories. You form mental images that are soothing to you and use it for relaxation of your mind. It is always preferred to try to use as much senses as possible such as sounds, textures, smells and sights.

- Mantra meditation. Usually used for over-coming negative thoughts. You repeatedly remember an event or otherwise repeat a certain word or phrase quite a few times with a positive mind-frame.

- Mindfulness meditation. It is when you focus so high that you can feel your breath. When you observe your emotions, thoughts and let them pass as they want to. That's when you really broaden your conscious awareness.

Qi gong. It is pronounced as CHEE-gung and is a traditional Chinese medicine. This is a combination of physical movements, breathing and relaxation exercises.

Tai chi. A form of Chinese martial arts where you perform different postures at a slow pace for practicing deep breathing and relaxation.

Yoga. To keep the focus on balance, concentration while you're engaged is improving your flexibility and working your way towards a calm mind.

CHAPTER 10

LEARN HOW TO TRICK THE MIND AND BECOME A BETTER PERSON

There is a better person in all of us and they are waiting to come out. This is especially true if you are suffering from a lot of bad behavioural patterns or need to kick a few undesirable habits that are detrimental to your health. Being a better person doesn't always mean being better for others, but it also means changing and stopping yourself from doing the things that could potentially wreck your life or hold you back from experiencing the successes that you deserve. Let us take ambition for an example.

Some of us have an immense drive and energy to constantly improve ourselves and some of us do not. For the latter, we are quite content to work on the things that life hands to us and view the top of the mountain as a waste of effort and energy. We normally have low energy levels and often recluse ourselves, subjecting our lives to a monotony of circular activities that have no benefit to us at all. Comfortable with the familiar and insecure with new changes. What about if we have a bad habit like smoking and drinking? There is no physical need for these activities but the mind often tells us that we need to perform them to serve a function and make us feel good. The problem with the world today is that they view nicotine and alcohol as drugs that are purely causing the addiction driving these two industries. I would argue that they are not.

I would say that it is the experience of smoking and drinking and what we associate it with that drive us to do it more and more. It is the feeling of comfort, ease, relaxation and loss of stress that we experience that is more addictive that the actual substance itself. Addiction is a sensory application that we need to recognise, and blaming a chemical compound will get us nowhere. Mental associations are very powerful forces indeed because they are rooted in the subconscious and they reproduce sensory stimulants/memory that cause us to re enact these moments through our bad habits. It becomes so routine that the mind releases chemical reactions before, during and even after the process so that we crave, we are satisfied and we crave some more.

What do you get when you combine the two? A person with no ambition and one who is driven to death with his addictions. The mind is tricking you and it is time to fight fire with fire. Science and the personal development industry has stepped in and given us the tools that we need to fight the persuasions rooted in the cerebral cortex. Binaural beats, subliminal messages, autogenics and biofeedback are just some of the technologies that are available from medicine and science - for the end user to make use of. Become a better person by attacking the root of the problem - and soon you will see a change in yourself like never before. Trick the mind and become a better person today with brainwave entrainment technology.

10 KEY POINTS TO BE A BETTER PERSON

Our personal character is what makes you different from the others. There are times that you seem to be bored of what you are, and you would like to undergo a change in your behavioral attributes to make you a new person, right? You may look into the following pointers so you could be a better person.

1. First thing that you should consider is being true to yourself. You should know yourself that much to be able to get a grasp on why you need to change. Every individual has his or her own strengths, as well as weaknesses. If you would be able to evaluate on this, then it's going to be a good start for you. First thing that you need to administer here, is some room from improvement. Your weaknesses are your gauge to improve.

2. It is necessary for you to have a positive outlook in life. There are times that change is not the answer to your problems. If it is not possible for you to accomplish one thing, it doesn't mean that you are a failure here. What you can do is to work on the possible things you can do first, and then move on to the complex tasks. Some things may be challenging for you but if you work on it with a smile, you will definitely succeed.

3. You probably have heard this several times already, "change is the only thing that is constant in this life on earth," so you better be open to a lot of changes. Anybody who fears change is not open for development, if that is the case, then there is no use to go on from here, right?

4. You have to give your best in everything that you do. If you strive for excellence, then that is the key to your success in life. If you want to be a better person, you should start doing things the right way, no excuses. You have to be result-oriented at all times, so you can provide superior results to the tasks that would be given to you.

5. Now, it is necessary for you to understand, that even perfectionists fail. If there are any mistakes that you have done with previous projects, learn from them, but do not think that you are a "loser." Most of the time we learn from our mistakes and that is not a bad thing. However, after learning from it, you have to bear in mind, that you shouldn't be performing the same mistake again.

6. You should be persistent in learning more about what you don't know. You have to develop your personality, and to do this you need to know more about yourself and what you are capable of doing. Adding more intellectual knowledge would be the best asset that you can keep with you all through your life.

7. Aside from knowledge, you would as well need to communicate effectively, this is a skill that everybody should be able to attain. Your communication skills would include active listening, concise writing, speaking clearly, as well as displaying an appropriate body language. Communicating effectively would bring you success to whatever endeavors you have in the future.

8. It is important that you learn to value others the same way, you value yourself. This is how you build relationships that are long lasting. You have to keep in mind that in developing your personality, you need to involve others to evaluate how far have you come .

9. Of course after all, you would need to make sure that you are happy with what you are doing. If you have accomplished anything at present, give yourself a little of that self appreciation it needs, this would enlighten your spirit and think more positively.

10. Lastly, be honest with yourself and with everything that you do. If you would like to gain respect from the people around you, you can earn that respect from having practicing integrity.

CHAPTER 11

A MONTHLY TRIP TO A BEAUTY SALON CAN MAKE YOU A BETTER PERSON

There are plenty of reasons for visiting a beauty salon regularly. People who are concerned about their overall look, health, fitness and personality may like to enjoy the advantages of visiting a salon. There are numerous advantages of visiting the day spa or getting some spa treatments. A person can be completely transformed into a new person not only by the way he or she looks but in terms of health and fitness also. Given below are some of the most important advantages of going to a beauty salon.

Skin is a very important part of our body. Since it is a visible part it has to be taken care of properly. If you are a busy person you may not have enough time to do all that is required for your skin. There are numerous types of treatments and methods for making your skin glow and look vibrant at the beauty salon. When you visit the beauty salon, the professionals know to give the right kind of treatment according to your skin type. So all you have to do is tell them what you require. They will suggest a number of ways to make your skin look glowing and vibrant.

Hair care is also one of the most important aspects of personal style. If the hair is healthy and beautiful it adds to the overall personality of the person. Just like your skin the hair also has a number of treatments for various problems. Only the experts will be able to recommend the right kind of treatment needed for your hair. So you can simply relax and enjoy the treatment. Another advantage of visiting the beauty salon is that they help you with a number of hair styles. If you have to attend a special function or an event you can take the help of the professionals at the beauty salon and style your hair accordingly. You can be the centre of attraction.

Visiting a beauty salon is one of the best ways to relax and get rid of your stress. The salons offer various kinds of massage services that are meant for various purposes. Most of the massage therapies can help you to improve your health, boost your overall energy and strengthen your body. If you have been busy for a long time, the best way to pamper your body is to get a massage done. There are different kinds of massages to choose from. Apart from beauty salons most of the tourist resorts in you locality will usually have this kind of spa treatments for the visitors.

The best part of visiting a beauty salon is that you can learn a lot of new things that are useful for taking care of your body and health. You can know the type of skin you have, the requirements of your hair and how to take care of many other aspects. You can also speak to the experts there and know about various things concerned with health and fashion. When you are equipped with the knowledge on the latest trends, you will be able to use these in your day-to-day life. This will help to become a better person altogether. So, find time to visit a beauty salon and transform yourself into a better person.

THINK BEFORE YOU SPEAK - IT WILL MAKE YOU A BETTER PERSON

Would you like to become a better person? Then think before you speak. If you do, you will certainly develop good relationships with people.

So, how can thinking before speaking help you become a better person?

1. If you practice thinking before speaking, you will not make a hasty and careless remark that you will regret later. This is probably the best and most practical advice that you can give to yourself.

2. When you make a careless remark, the hurtful or offensive words that you say to anyone will haunt you forever. Always remind yourself that you can never bring back the damage caused by those hurtful words that you don't mean to say in the first place.

3. If someone says something hurtful behind your back, verify the truth and politely request for an explanation from the source. Never think of retaliating by throwing the same offensive words and ignite the fire. Don't be the kind of person who will stoop down to anyone's level.

4. In moments when you are tempted to say something hurtful or offensive in front of anyone - better stop and hold your tongue. We have long learned from our elders that we should never humiliate anyone and it is better not to say anything than say something stupid and worthless, anyway. Practice this elderly advice and you will surely feel good about yourself. Most of the time, it is best to keep your silence when you are angry because when you speak in anger, you will only make a fool of yourself.

. In times when you would feel like gossiping or saying something negative about anyone, better hold your tongue as well. You do not have any idea how much paranoia it can get you later on.

Think before you speak. Practice tact in every conversation and make less or no enemies. That will surely make you become a better person.

CONCLUSION

Always be positive towards yourself stop the negative self talk. We all have thousands of thoughts that run through our heads on a daily basis, most of those can be negative if we do not learn how to control our thoughts. You must take control of the thoughts and learn how to replace the negative thoughts with positive affirmations. Constantly fill your subconscious with things like I am successful, I am powerful, everything I desire is on its way to me, I am creative, etc... As you continue to do this on a daily basis you will influence your subconscious mind and before long you will become a better you.

You must begin today to form better habits in order to become a better you. If you desire anything in life you must learn how to get rid of some bad habits and begin developing new habits. It takes 30 days to develop a new habit; yet most people do not have the self discipline to stick with it until it does become a habit. Once you get past the 30 days something becomes routine and you do not have to think about it anymore. If you wish to begin working on a new habit take small steps towards achieving it; however begin at once.

Printed in Great Britain
by Amazon